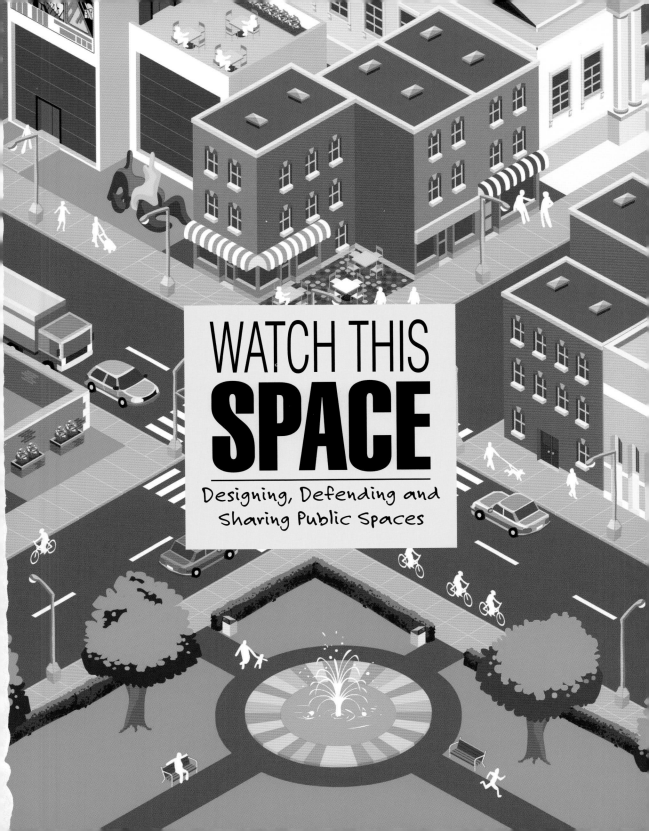

WATCH THIS SPACE

Designing, Defending and Sharing Public Spaces

For Adam Dyer, lego wizard — H.D.

To Zoey, Jack and Arin — M.N.

Kids Can Press acknowledges the financial support of the Government of Ontario, through the Ontario Media Development Corporation's Ontario Book Initiative; the Ontario Arts Council; the Canada Council for the Arts; and the Government of Canada, through the BPIDP, for our publishing activity.

Published in Canada by
Kids Can Press Ltd.
29 Birch Avenue
Toronto, ON M4V 1E2

Published in the U.S. by
Kids Can Press Ltd.
2250 Military Road
Tonawanda, NY 14150

www.kidscanpress.com

Kids Can Press is a _orus_™ Entertainment company

Edited by Karen Li
Designed by Karen Powers

Printed and bound in China
This book is smyth sewn casebound.

CM 10 0 9 8 7 6 5 4 3 2 1

Library and Archives Canada Cataloguing in Publication

Dyer, Hadley

    Watch this space : designing, defending and sharing public spaces / written by Hadley Dyer ; illustrated by Marc Ngui.

Includes index.

ISBN 978-1-55453-293-3

1. Public spaces—Juvenile literature.
2. Public spaces—Social aspects—Juvenile literature. I. Ngui, Marc, 1972– II. Title.

HT152.D94 2010   j307.1'216   C2009-903895-1

WATCH THIS
SPACE

Designing, Defending and Sharing Public Spaces

Written by Hadley Dyer

Illustrated by Marc Ngui

KIDS CAN PRESS

contents

Introduction

When I was a teenager living in rural Nova Scotia, there were two places kids spent most of their time when they weren't at school: the McDonald's parking lot and a gigantic sand pit. I have no recollection of what we did there. Not much, I guess. Talked. Laughed. Argued. Checked people out. Like today, when I ask a teen what he does when he's on-line all night, he'll usually just shrug. "Hang out."

Around the world, youth hang out in public spaces and adults wish they wouldn't. People wonder, Why do they have to be so loud? Why are there always so many of them? When teens take over little-used or abandoned spaces, such as a parking lot, people get even more nervous. Why are they hanging out *there*? What exactly are they getting up to?

The answer is often nothing. Unlike adults, teens don't have private places to call their own. At home, parents decide who can come over, when they have to leave, how

loud the music can be. At school, teachers are always keeping a watchful eye. That's why it was such a big deal when McDonald's arrived in my town. It gave us someplace to go. To see and be seen. To be together. To do, well, nothing.

Yet something *is* happening when you spend time in public spaces. You're figuring out how to get along with people, without adult interference. You're sorting out who you are and how you fit in. You're becoming part of a community.

Of course, teens aren't teens forever. So this book is about why public space is important — and not just for people who have nowhere else to go. We want you to become passionate about public space because you can help save it and fight for its future, long after you stop just hanging out. There are many reasons why you should care about public space, but the most compelling one is this: you will always need it. And it belongs to you, too.

"I see people in the park forgetting their troubles and woes
They're drinking and dancing, wearing bright colored clothes
All the young men with their young women looking so good
Well, I'd trade places with any of them in a minute, if I could."
— Bob Dylan, "Highlands"

What is
public space?

You don't have to buy something or pay an entry fee to be in a public space. You don't need to be a member or explain why you're there. Public spaces exist so everyone can use them. All you have to do is show up.

What is **public space**?

Sitting quietly,
    doing nothing,
Spring comes,
    and the grass grows
by itself.

— Zen proverb

So, what is public space, exactly? It is a place that anyone may enter freely — young or old, rich or poor. Public spaces belong to everyone and to no one in particular. Think of public parks, public gardens and public beaches. The word "public" means these spaces are owned by the people, not privately owned by individuals or companies. Town squares are public spaces and so are the streets and sidewalks under your feet. Public spaces also include buildings, such as civic centers and libraries.

Public spaces are gathering places. They are places to meet up with friends. They are where we have chance encounters with neighbors and strangers. In public spaces you may come to know people you might otherwise never talk to.

It's not the size of a public space that makes it valuable, it's the way it's used. Some have a specific function — say, buying food at an outdoor market or washing clothes in a river. Playgrounds provide kids with a place to exercise and explore. Likewise, urban dogs need off-leash parks where they can run and play.

We go to public spaces to celebrate cultural traditions and watch special events, be it the colorful Mardi Gras Parade in New Orleans or a royal procession outside Buckingham Palace. They may have symbolic importance, such as the Vietnam Veterans Memorial Wall in Washington, DC.

Some public spaces are used for nothing more than to get away from the frantic pace of everyday life. Even when a place is crowded and busy, you will find people who seem to be alone with their thoughts. Public spaces provide a retreat where you can enjoy the scenery, a piece of art or a hot dog. Whether or not we seek out other people, we are participating in public life by just being there. Public spaces are the places we go to watch the world go by.

The Ganges River, which runs through Nepal, India and Bangladesh, is a holy place in the Hindu religion. It is also the main source of water for many of the 350 million people who live along its banks.

In cities such as Varanasi, the riverbank is packed with people bathing, washing their clothes and collecting drinking water as fisherman and travelers pass by.

Every twelve years, Hindu pilgrims wash away their sins in the river during the Maha Kumbh Mela, or Grand Pitcher Festival. In 2003, 70 million people attended — so many, the crowds were visible from space!

The Ganges is polluted from overuse, but most of the people who rely on it have no alternative water sources. Many become ill from using water that has been contaminated with sewage and waste products from factories.

11

Is it a **public** space?

How do you know you're entering a public space? Ask yourself two questions:

1. Who owns it?

Public spaces are usually owned and managed by governments, which means they belong to the people of a city, province, state or country. (That means you, by the way.) Some public spaces are owned by nonprofit organizations but receive funding from governments to support public use of the space.

2. Who may enter it?

A true public space is open to all people — whether they live locally or are strangers from afar. Ideally, there is no fee for admission so that anyone can afford to use the space.

Sounds simple enough? It can get a bit confusing. Take military bases, for example. Although they're owned by the government, they are definitely not open to just anyone. Military bases may be public property, but not all public property is a public space. There are also many places that appear to be open to anyone, such as cafés or bowling alleys, but are privately owned. These may be social spaces — meaning, they bring people together — but they aren't true public spaces.

☑ **Museum**
Many museums and galleries are publicly owned, but there may be a fee for entry.

☑ **Public school**
Usually, the general public isn't permitted to enter a school without permission, but school auditoriums, gymnasiums, libraries and grounds are often used as public space outside of school hours.

☑ **Sidewalk**

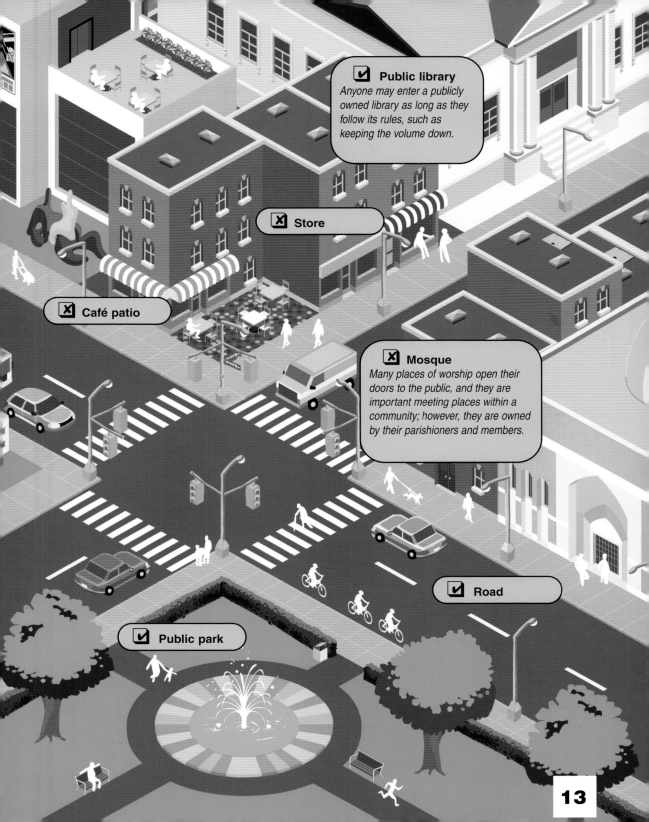

✔ **Public library**
Anyone may enter a publicly owned library as long as they follow its rules, such as keeping the volume down.

✘ Store

✘ Café patio

✘ **Mosque**
Many places of worship open their doors to the public, and they are important meeting places within a community; however, they are owned by their parishioners and members.

✔ Road

✔ Public park

Are **malls** public spaces?

Malls look a lot like public spaces. They have paths for foot traffic, where people stop to talk to one another. They include places to rest or have a bite to eat. Some even have gardens, waterfalls and art exhibits.

Although malls and other retail centers may function like public spaces, they aren't the real deal. Ever notice that you rarely see homeless people snoozing on benches at the mall like you might at the park? That's because mall security would be quick to kick them out. Ultimately, it's up to the people who own and manage a shopping center to decide who may enter it and how the space will be used.

For example, more than fifty malls across the United States now have curfews for teens. According to a 2007 study, 54% of teenaged boys and 75% of teenaged girls had spent one or more hours at the mall in the past seven days. Curfews help shopping centers get rid of these "mallrats."

MALL WARS

In 1993, Jasmine McCoy, then 18, found herself spending a lot of time at the mall. She wasn't shopping — she was working with the Buncombe County Youth Organizing Project in Asheville, North Carolina, to protest a new curfew for teens at the Asheville Mall. Kids under the age of 16 were no longer allowed to enter the mall after 6:00 p.m. unless accompanied by an adult. Teens were also banned from assembling in groups of more than four and not permitted to wear bandanas because of their association with gang culture. Malls are privately owned, so they can set the rules, but Jasmine and her friends weren't going to put up with age discrimination.

The youth activists held meetings at schools to gather support for their protest. They distributed flyers and met with mall management. They won some battles: the mall dropped its restrictions on groups of teens and bandanas. But with more and more malls imposing curfews, it seems teens are losing the war.

Mall management argues that packs of unruly teens intimidate paying customers and clash with one another. The Mall of America in Bloomington, Minnesota, one of the first malls to introduce curfews, claims that violent incidents at the mall dropped from 300 per year to just two after its curfew was put into place.

Those shopping centers that don't have curfews point out that cut-off times for youth are discriminatory. Curfews may also discourage teens who actually want to shop. After all, in the United States alone, teens have a spending power of more than 150 billion dollars per year.

Early public spaces

The idea that people need public space is hardly new. In ancient Greece, way back in the sixth century BCE, the "agora" was the center of public life in Athens. The word referred to both an assembly of people and the physical space where they gathered. (Today, "agoraphobia" means a fear of public or open spaces.) The agora was originally a simple square defined by boundary stones. Over the next 400 years, it became a place for trading goods, theatrical performances, athletic contests and political events. The majestic Altar of the Twelve Gods was the most important religious monument in the agora and marked the exact center of Athens.

In 146 BCE, the Romans conquered the Greeks, and Greece became part of the Roman Empire. The Roman "forum" — Latin for "open space" or "marketplace" — was very similar to the agora, and was the center of political and religious activities. Rome had several such centers, but the most prominent was the *Forum Romanum*, or, simply, the Roman Forum.

The Romans constructed many buildings for public life, such as bathhouses for bathing and circuses for chariot racing. Using improved building materials and new techniques, the Romans left an astounding architectural legacy, where the spaces created were as impressive as the grand arches and domes that marked them.

NOW THAT'S ENTERTAINMENT

Imagine you're a slave in Rome around 80 BCE. Your owner tells you he'd like to send you for some "athletic training." Uh-oh.

Throughout the Roman Empire, professional and amateur gladiators fought each other or wild animals to entertain the enthusiastic fans who crowded into public amphitheaters. Many gladiators were criminals, slaves and prisoners of war who had zero choice about fighting to the death.

Sick, right? But how many people packed theaters to see the Oscar-winning movie version? The truth is people love a spectacle, from the glory of the Olympic Games (the first of which was held in 776 BCE) to the solemn drama of public executions. From about 1400 to 1700 CE, tens of thousands of people accused of witchcraft were burned at the stake in Europe, often while their neighbors looked on. In the United States, at least 20 000 people witnessed the country's last public execution in 1936.

4000 – 1000 BCE

Public parks and gardens may date as far back as the Sumerians (4000–2000 BCE), the earliest known civilization in the world, and ancient Babylon (1000 BCE). The grounds are owned by royalty but made available to the people.

64 CE

In Israel, the high priest Yehoshua Ben Gamla decrees that all Jewish boys over the age of five must gather to study regardless of family wealth, creating one of the earliest versions of pubic school.

300 BCE – 400 CE

The Great Library of Alexandria opens in Egypt. Public libraries appear in Greece around the fourth century BCE and continue to flourish under the Romans.

1420s

The Gate of Heavenly Peace, the front entrance into the Imperial City in Beijing, China, is constructed. It will later become part of Tiananmen Square, the largest open urban square in the world.

1634

Boston Common, the first public park in the United States, is established, although it won't be used for recreational purposes until the mid-1800s. Instead, like other commons of the period, it's used for grazing cattle (and the occasional public hanging).

1833

In England, the Select Committee on Public Walks reports that urban parks promote health through contact with nature and ease stress in crowded cities.

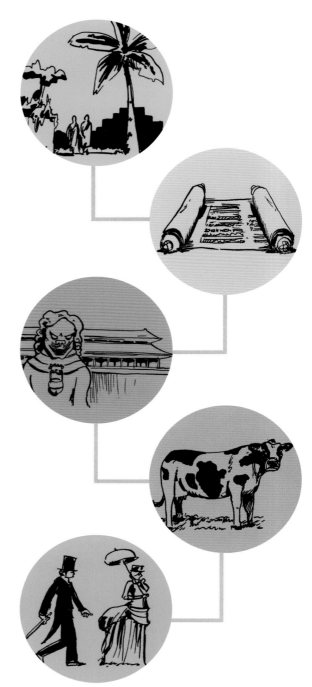

1863

The first tube line of the London Underground opens, launching the world's first subway system.

1873

New York's Central Park, the first landscaped park — and today the most visited urban park — in the United States officially opens. It was designed by landscape architect Frederick Law Olmsted, the founder of American landscape architecture, and architect Calvert Vaux.

1895

Local transit takes a leap forward in Mannheim, Germany, when eight passengers climb aboard the first engine-powered bus, designed by Karl Benz (who later put the Benz in Mercedes-Benz).

1916

National Park Service in the United States is created. It oversees more than 400 natural, recreational and cultural sites, including the Everglades, the Grand Canyon and the Statue of Liberty.

1972

The United Nations Educational, Scientific and Cultural Organization (UNESCO) establishes the World Heritage programs, which identify and help preserve sites of natural and cultural importance around the world, from the Serengeti National Park in Tanzania to the Historic District of Old Quebec in Canada.

Stuck in the zone

In 1922, the first shopping mall, Country Club Plaza, opened near Kansas City. It catered to a new lifestyle development that would change North America: the suburbs.

Cities are high-density, built upward, with lots of people living and working close together. Suburbs are low density, built outward. They have shorter buildings with much more space between them. Because the suburbs sprawl over vast areas of land, life is divided into different zones: home, work, shopping, recreation, worship. Houses are clustered in subdivisions. Workers commute into the city or business parks. Shopping requires a trip to a big box store or the mall.

So how does suburban sprawl affect youth? If you're a teen who lives in one of the newer subdivisions where there aren't any sidewalks, let alone parks, you know the answer. Without a car, you're stuck in your zone. In a city, you may wander up the street to buy a soda or swing by the library on a whim. In the suburbs, you

usually have a specific reason for leaving your zone, because you'll need to be driven wherever you go. (And you'll probably head somewhere that has a parking lot.) All this driving means fewer places to participate in public life, fewer places where you can just show up and hang out, and that means less independence and freedom.

No wonder teens spend so much time at the mall.

"The adolescent houseguest, I would suggest, is probably the best and quickest test of the vitality of a neighborhood; the visiting teenager in the subdivision soon acts like an animal in a cage ... There is no place to which they can escape and join their own kind."

— Ray Oldenburg, sociologist

Federation Square is the heart of art and culture in Melbourne, Australia. Surrounded by a creative mix of public and private attractions, it hosts more than 2000 events annually, ensuring a steady stream of tourists and locals.

The square was built on a massive concrete deck over busy railway lines.

People enjoy sun, shade and outdoor Wi-Fi next to contemporary buildings made of sandstone, zinc and glass.

The square can hold 15 000 people, whether for cultural festivals, concerts, outdoor markets or protests. Cultural centers include the Australian Centre for the Moving Images and the Melbourne Visitor Centre.

22

Finding **new** common ground

Does zone living mean the end of public life? It doesn't have to. Although we may retreat into our private spaces at night, consider this: where do we go from there? More and more, people head directly to the computer and toward new, rapidly developing types of social spaces, such as the Internet.

But is the Internet a public space? Well, sort of.

From its earliest days, the Internet has been referred to as an "information commons," a place to gather and exchange information, ideas and goods. As in the village commons of yore, you're always bumping into people on-line, which has its benefits (faraway friends) and risks (predators lurking in chat rooms). But the Internet doesn't always fit the definition of public space. Consider our first standard: who owns it? Governments have invested a lot of money in developing the Internet, but so has the private sector. About 83% of Web sites are commercial, or owned by businesses.

And what about our second standard: who may enter the Internet? Not everyone can afford their own computer and Internet connection, although libraries provide Internet service for free. Access also depends on where you want to go. Commercial Web sites can control site traffic by requiring members to register and sometimes pay a fee.

On the other hand, you can roam freely in cyberspace. There are no teachers, librarians and parents to censor what you read. Even content control programs, such as Net Nanny, can filter out only a relatively small percentage of sites, and many teens know how to get around them. A kid living in a dead-end zone might not have a lot of places to go in his neighborhood, but the whole world is his when he connects to the Internet.

Virtual social spaces

Social networking Web sites, such as Facebook, Myspace and YouTube, have become important gathering places where you can hang out with friends and meet new people, too. (Although research has shown that teens' on-line social groups usually aren't wildly different than their real-life friends.) These virtual communities offer a combination of services, including blogs, e-mail, chatrooms and places to post images, music clips and videos.

Like the mall, social networking spaces seem a lot like public spaces but are privately owned, and they are carefully designed to attract a certain crowd. Once you enter a social networking site, your every move may be watched, although not by mall cops. Marketers use these sites to collect useful information about young consumers, such as your favorite brands, and advertisers pay a lot of money to advertise on them.

But for every savvy marketer, there are others using the Internet to fight for and promote public spaces. For instance, a nonprofit collective called Murmur Inc. has created real and virtual walking tours of several cities, including Galway, San Jose, Edinburgh and Toronto. Print a map from the Murmur Web site and head off with your mobile phone in search of one of the ear-shaped signs that have phone numbers printed on them. Once found, call the number to listen to a story about the exact place you are standing. Or, you can click on the map on-line to listen to the audio recording from home.

YOU TOO

The swiftness with which social networking sites take off is breathtaking. Facebook, for example, launched in February 2004 and had 57 million members by the end of 2007. YouTube went live in February 2005. In July 2006, the company revealed that more than 100 million videos were being watched on the Web site every day. In November of that same year, Google Inc. acquired YouTube for $1.65 billion (US) in Google stock. Why are these companies worth so much? Because they have your attention! Like it or not, you're being used for market research and helping companies sell their products every time you log in.

Sharing
public spaces

"Hey, watch it!" On your way to school, you're practically pushed off the
sidewalk by a herd of sweaty joggers. Great, your
sneaker landed in doggie doo. Back on concrete,
you just miss getting sideswiped by a cyclist. You
turn around to yell — wait a sec, he's kind of cute!
What school does he go to?

Retro living

I used to live on Montrose Avenue in Little Portugal, a residential neighborhood in downtown Toronto, one of the world's most multicultural cities. When I moved into my flat, my landlord said, "Don't put your bike in the garage. Chain it to the fence next to the sidewalk. It's safer there."

Montrose was never deserted. Every morning, the old women emerged in their housedresses to hose down the front walks. Their husbands spent all day inside cafes and on the benches that lined the storefronts in nearby Little Italy. In the afternoon, kids biked up and down the street, and families hung out on their porches after supper. After everyone else had gone to bed, young guys would lean on their cars and drink coffee until the wee hours. (As far as I could tell, they only talked about cars, all night long.)

It was like living on a 1950s movie set — from the post-war houses to the feeling of being in front of a camera all the time. If someone had a new girlfriend or took a trip, everyone knew it. I could walk to a corner store at midnight and never be alone.

Sure, there were times when I needed to pull down the shades and put in earphones (the street was especially noisy with chatter on summer evenings), but Little Portugal was one of the safest places I have ever lived. And my bike, parked right next to Montrose Avenue, was never stolen.

Better **together**

Back in 1961, when the suburbs were booming, sociologist Jane Jacobs started ringing the alarm. The dream of suburban life was flawed, she warned in her revolutionary book *Death and Life of Great American Cities*.

The suburbs promised so much. Far from the jumble and noise of cities, they offered tidy, crime-free streets and lots of space. Your neighbors would all be middle class, just like you. They would live in houses just like yours, and life would be predictable and safe.

But when everyone retreats into their private spaces, a hush falls over the suburbs. Gone is the vibrancy of urban living. People have no reason to use sidewalks that lead nowhere. The police can't patrol every street in such spread-out neighborhoods, and so abandoned streets can become dangerous streets.

By contrast, Jacobs argued, busy streets are self-policing. At any given time there are many eyes on the street — shopkeepers and doormen, people running errands, neighbors chatting and kids playing. Jacobs proposed a return to the old "togetherness": high-density streets with a variety of uses. That's what attracts people, and lots of them. The more strangers, the merrier, she claimed.

STRANGER DANGER

Don't talk to strangers. It's one of the first lessons we learn. Studies show that parents believe the world is becoming increasingly dangerous for their children. In fact, kids are significantly more likely to be abducted by someone they know, such as a parent who has been fighting for custody. The number of children kidnapped or killed by strangers every year remains relatively small and hasn't changed significantly in decades. Statistically, childhood deaths are most likely to occur in public spaces, but not at the hands of child predators. The number one killer of people under the age of eighteen is traffic accidents.

Laws and limits

All societies have rules that guide our behavior in shared space and help us get along with one another. The rules of etiquette tell us that one should not pick one's nose at the bus stop. Good manners require us to be pleasant and courteous to others. Taboos are things that people are forbidden from saying or doing because society considers them unacceptable. What one culture finds harmless, such as hand-holding, another culture might consider improper, even dangerous. No one in particular enforces these rules. As we grow up, our parents and friends teach us what's okay and what is not.

Other rules are set down in law and enforced, usually by police. Many public space laws were created to keep people safe. They also help ensure that no one infringes on another person's enjoyment of a space. For example, you can't smoke cigarettes in most public buildings because secondhand smoke is both annoying and downright dangerous to the nonsmokers exposed to it.

The fairness of a law may depend on what side of it you're on. You might be glad there are noise restriction bylaws when you're studying for an exam, but they can be a drag when you're having a house party.

Public space **offenders**

Public behavior laws can make it easier to share space by legally enforcing common courtesy. Laws differ widely from one place to the next, so do your homework before you wander into a public space abroad!

• In Paris, the smart *piéton* (pedestrian) keeps an eye on his feet because the sidewalks are a minefield of *déjections canines*. (Do you really need a translation?) Although the French are famous for not picking up after their pooches, there is indeed a law that says everyone except the visually impaired has to pick up after their dogs.

• Lawmakers in Beijing prepared for the 2008 Summer Olympic Games by targeting the manners of the local citizenry. In China, public spitting isn't as frowned upon as elsewhere. But under new city bylaws, those who are caught depositing phlegm in a public space will have to deposit a fine, too.

• Singapore has stringent anti-littering laws. Those who smuggle gum, the scourge of sidewalks, into the country risk a year in jail and a fine of about $5500 (US). Drop a piece of trash, and you could get nailed for $1000 and be sentenced to picking up garbage for no pay.

• In 2004, France banned students from wearing obvious religious symbols to public schools. The government says the law is necessary to keep public schools secular (totally non-religious). In addition to the hijab — the headscarf worn by Muslim girls and women — students are forbidden to wear Jewish skullcaps, Sikh turbans and obvious Christian crosses.

• Have your parents ever made you change your clothes before you go out? Parental rules aside, most countries have laws that determine how much of the human body can be exposed in public. Genitals must be covered just about everywhere. Unlike men, women can go shirtless in some places and not others. (You might be surprised to learn women can legally drop their tops in Canada.) Several Islamic countries have adopted a very strict interpretation of the Shariah Laws, a code of living for devout Muslims. In those countries, men must be clothed from knee to waist and women are completely covered except for their faces and hands.

• How much is too much when it comes to public displays of affection (PDAs)? In Rome, the nuns don't bat an eyelash at the couples canoodling on the crowded Spanish Steps, one of the world's great public spaces. In South Africa, teens launched a Facebook campaign to protest a law that bans youth from kissing in public.

Big Brother is watching

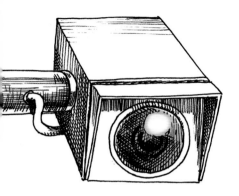

How often are your movements and actions recorded in public space each day? In the United Kingdom, the average person is recorded on Closed Circuit Television (CCTV) surveillance cameras more than 300 times per day! Some research has shown that while neighborhoods may experience a dip in crime rates after new cameras are installed, the trouble simply moves on to another area. Is the high cost of surveillance and the infringement on your right to privacy worth the temporary sense of security?

"When you go home at night, you probably close the blinds. It's not because you're trying to hide something. You just instinctively need your privacy, your freedom from being observed ... This essential human need, and fundamental right, is in danger of slipping away from us. And once it's lost, it will be very, very hard to get it back ... I know that some people say, 'What's the harm? So there's a camera — big deal.' In fact, in Kelowna [British Columbia] one of the business leaders was quoted as saying that having cameras everywhere would be no different than having a police officer on every corner and nobody could object to that. Well, there are places in the world where there's a police officer on every corner. They're called police states. That's not the way we do things in Canada."

— George Radwanski, former Privacy Commissioner of Canada, in a speech to the British Columbia Branch of the Canadian Bar Association

Are you ready for your close-up? You might be surprised at the number of cameras keeping watch in your neighborhood, often cleverly disguised or hidden from view.

Space invaders

The TV show *Seinfeld* introduced the phrase "close talker" to describe someone who gets too close for comfort while you're having a conversation. Personal space is the amount of room someone needs between themselves and others. Most people avoid sitting next to someone they don't know unless there are no other seats available. We avert eye contact on subways, using newspapers like armor and iPods to tune people out. Darkness also provides a buffer. In fact, once the lights go down, we may even enjoy the closeness of others in a darkened movie theater or dance floor. But think of how odd and uncomfortable you feel when the lights go up again.

Not all cultures place equal value on personal space. In North America, where people from all over the world live together, occasional conflicts are inevitable. In the 1960s, anthropologist Edward T. Hall developed the theory of proxemics — how people communicate through their proximity, or closeness, to each other. He measured the average distance Americans required from another person in order to feel comfortable and came up with the measurements below.

Personal space
(casual conversation):
90 cm (3 ft.) in every direction

Intimate space
(highly personal conversation):
15 to 46 cm (6 to 18 in.)

Social space
(business meeting):
1 to 4 m (3 to 13 ft.)

Recently, United Kingdom researchers have noted that we maintain these spaces even in virtual life. They released a specially designed avatar (virtual alter-ego) into the Internet game *Second Life*. The avatar stood too close to the avatars of other participants, causing them to move away to regain their personal space.

Public space
(between an audience and speaker):
4 to 8 m (13 to 26 ft.)

SAYING NO TO SEXUAL HARASSMENT

Your personal space can be invaded from afar, too. Cisnell Baez and Ashley Cotton, both 17, were already active members of two youth affairs committees in Boston when they decided they'd heard too many wolf whistles. Fellow female committee members complained that whenever they attended meetings on Centre Street, in Boston's Jamaica Plain neighborhood, they had to walk past men who whistled and called out to them. After undergoing training in how to deal with sexual harassment, the 17-year-old activists created the Campaign Against Sexual Harassment. Through theater workshops, information cards distributed on the street, a rally and a press conference with local media, they delivered a clear message to would-be harassers: Enough is enough.

Are you willing to **share** your **space** with anyone?

Keeping the peace in public space taps into big issues, like tolerance, equality and rights. Public space advocates complain that many laws unfairly target certain groups of people and that the police enforce laws more strictly with some people than others. The most commonly targeted groups? The homeless, panhandlers, youth and activists.

Imagine a woman sitting on a bench in a city park, shopping bags at her feet, cup of coffee in her hand. A nice picture of someone enjoying a public space, isn't it?

Now imagine those bags contain all of the woman's worldly possessions. The coffee cup has a few coins inside and a note scratched on the side that reads, "Please help." Many people would no longer share a bench with this woman. Some might say she has ruined their own enjoyment of the park and made them feel unsafe.

Like teens, the homeless need public spaces because they have no private spaces of their own. But for those without homes, the situation is far more desperate. While teens seek out places to be independent, a homeless person needs a place to sleep. Many complain that shelters are overcrowded and dangerous. Others don't like feeling at the mercy of those who run the shelter and being obliged to follow the shelter's rules.

In 2006, the United States Court of Appeals struck down the convictions of six people who had been arrested for sleeping on sidewalks and in other public spaces in Los Angeles, even though the local shelters were full. The Court cited the Eighth Amendment to the United States Constitution, which bars cruel and unusual punishment. In his ruling, the judge noted that "involuntary sitting, lying or sleeping on public sidewalks … is an unavoidable consequence of being human and homeless without shelter."

STREET YOUTH

Although many people pity the homeless, there is a persistent myth that homeless teens are giving the finger to authority and refusing to get jobs. In reality, many street youth come from abusive homes or struggle with addictions. A 2002 Canadian study revealed that almost 46% of homeless teens had been attacked in the past 12 months, compared to just over 6% of youth with homes. Another study found that street youth work an average of three jobs in a year. Not having a permanent address was the major obstacle to securing a permanent job.

Brother, can you **spare** a dime?

Panhandling — strangers asking you for money — can be upsetting, even scary if done aggressively. In response, cities have been creating bylaws that ban or restrict panhandling, especially near bank machines, restaurant patios, transit stops, pay phones and other places where people may feel cornered by the panhandler. Some cities have tried introducing panhandling permits, although they have proven difficult to administer.

Panhandling laws are designed to protect citizens from feeling disturbed or unsafe in public spaces. On the surface, this seems reasonable enough. But panhandling laws inevitably discriminate against people who suffer from poverty. After all, what are the odds the police will arrest a middle-class mom who asks for change outside the laundromat? Panhandling laws target our society's most vulnerable citizens. They choose the majority's right to not be disturbed over a minority's right to find a way to survive.

HOME SWEET HOME

In Osaka, Japan, parks and other public spaces are dotted with the blue plastic tarps of the *no jyuku sha*. Many of these "field campers" live in small tent villages on the banks of the Osaka River. They may not own the land they sleep on, but they don't consider themselves homeless. Web sites and blogs promote their cause as the city routinely evicts the tent-dwellers, using fences to make it difficult for them to return. Although the city has built shelters for the homeless, the *no jyuku sha* community does not see these heavily monitored environments as a good alternative to pitching a tent on a patch of green.

Ephebiphobia (Fear of youth)

Teenagers often find themselves at the center of conflicts over shared space. They're among the most likely to have limits placed on their use of it, such as mall curfews. Some cities even have curfews that banish youth from the streets at nighttime. (Imagine trying to get home from a hockey game or your part-time job in a place like that.) Many loitering laws were designed specifically to keep kids from lingering in public spaces.

While it's true that some youth crimes, like vandalism and theft, tend to be committed at night, studies have shown that curfews don't have a consistent effect on those crime rates. So, why do some cities persist in discriminating against teens in public spaces? It all boils down to a stereotype: teenagers are rebellious. They don't like to play by the rules, and that makes them dangerous.

For many people, skateboarders embody everything that is scary about youth. Zipping along crowded streets or barreling down steps, they seem to have no regard for the law, let alone the rules of polite society. In the United Kingdom, the cities of Sheffield, Manchester and Cardiff have banned skateboarding from their entire city centers.

It is true that skateboarding causes problems for other people in public spaces. It can be noisy and disruptive, and it does real damage to public property. But aside from the possibility of scrapes and broken bones, skateboarding is much healthier than a lot of other things teens could be getting up to.

What if, instead of restricting or banning the sport, skateboarders had public spaces where they could do it right? What if cities and towns invited teens to help create spaces where they can feel like they belong?

SAFETY IN NUMBERS

Public spaces can be valuable training grounds for teens, places to learn how to be safe, independent and responsible. "People who want to drive kids out of public space have it backwards," says Dylan Reid, public space activist. "The more a space is used, the safer it is for everyone. It's better for teens to be with lots of other teens because there's safety in numbers."

Start by choosing your space wisely. Everyone is safer in well-lit, well-used public spaces. And it's never good when one social group dominates, so look for places where a variety of people hang out. By sticking together and using common sense, you can find safety in the company of both friends and strangers.

PEST CONTROL

For years, classical music has been blasted in parks and transit stations and outside stores. The old tunes seem to deter people from loitering and reduce drug transactions, muggings and other crimes. Now a Welsh inventor has developed new technology that specifically targets teens. On its Web site, the manufacturer asks, "Is your business suffering from antisocial youths driving your customers away or generally causing damage or nuisance? Are you bothered by crowds of teenagers hanging around your street and making life unpleasant?"

Well, look no further! The Mosquito emits a 17 kHz sound that drives teens away. Children and dogs don't appear to be bothered by it, and adults over the age of 25 can't hear it. But for teens, the whining sound becomes so irritating after a few minutes that they will move on to escape it.

Human rights groups have challenged the device, but it continues to grow in popularity. However, techno-savvy teens may have the last laugh. You can now download a cell phone ring tone that, like the Mosquito, emits a sound that is too high-pitched for parents and teachers to hear.

JFK Plaza in Philadelphia, Pennsylvania, is commonly known as Love Park (nicknamed for the "LOVE" sculpture by artist Robert Indiana). Its steps and the curved granite ledges surrounding its fountain used to be an irresistible draw for skateboarders. ESPN used the park for their 2001 and 2002 X-Games extreme sports competition.

Although some people credit skateboarders for driving drug dealers out of the area, the sport was banned from Love Park in 2002.

Today, strategically placed stone planters and trash cans discourage skateboarding, creating a more peaceful place for the general public.

Skatepark Westblaak

Before it was turned into the largest skateboarding park in the Netherlands, the center of Rotterdam was a dead zone of dreary, underused city streets. Skateboarders not only came up with the idea for the park, they helped design it and worked with the city to establish responsible ways to use and police it.

Opened in 2000, Skatepark Westblaak now features 6700 square meters (over 1½ acres) of adrenaline-pumping ramps, stainless steel obstacles and calming green spaces for chilling between stunts. It also provides a safe, fun place for young skaters to learn the sport.

Skatepark Westblaak hosts events throughout the year, like music concerts and break-dancing competitions. It attracts serious skateboarders from around the world, as well as ordinary civilians who just like watching the action.

Taking it to the **streets**

The principle of civil disobedience is that you sometimes have to break the rules in order to change the rules. Public spaces are often the sites of protests and other activism because you can grab the attention of many people who might otherwise never learn about your cause with signs, information materials and noise.

In Canada and the United States, your rights to protest are set out in the Canadian Charter of Rights and Freedoms and the United States Bill of Rights. They include the freedom of peaceful assembly and freedom of association. In other words, you have the right to get together with other people and join any group you wish. Additionally, you can't be searched, detained or imprisoned if you haven't broken any rules.

In France, public workers strike frequently, and protesters take over the streets by the hundreds of thousands. Though not everyone likes the disruption — some demonstrations have turned violent — protesting is an accepted part of French culture and political life. Not so elsewhere in the world. Here are a few history-making protests that took place in public spaces.

The space:

Tiananmen Square, Beijing, China

At almost half a square kilometer (more than 100 acres), it is the largest urban square in the world, able to contain one million people.

Lincoln Memorial, Washington, DC

Opened to the public in 1922, this 30.5-meter-high (100-foot-tall) monument to the 16th president was designed to look like a Greek temple.

The Berlin Wall, Berlin, Germany

Heavily guarded and covered with barbed wire, the Wall separated communist East Germany from democratic West Germany through the city of Berlin.

Piazza della Repubblica, Rome, Italy

Built in 1901, this historic square is home to the Fountain of the Naiads, sculpted by Mario Rutelli, and surrounded by the city's business district.

FIGHTING THE GOOD FIGHT

The cause:	The outcome:
On June 4, 1989, thousands of protestors, most of them students, marched for democratic reform in the communist state.	Police opened fire on the crowds, massacring hundreds. The government earned worldwide condemnation for the killings and for cracking down on further protests and the foreign press.
During the March on Washington for Jobs and Freedom in 1963, Martin Luther King, Jr., gave a rousing speech titled "I Have a Dream" — a defining moment of the American civil rights movement.	Congress sped up civil rights legislation, and King became the youngest recipient of the Nobel Peace Prize.
More than 2.5 million people fled East Germany after it became part of the Soviet Union following World War Two. When the wall was built in 1961, families, friends and neighbors were divided.	The Berlin Wall fell on November 9, 1989, and Germany was reunified.
On February 15, 2003, between one and three million Romans — along with six to ten million people worldwide — protested the United States' threats to invade Iraq.	The largest global anti-war rally in history failed to stop the United States from going to war with Iraq.

"Design is people."
— Jane Jacobs, writer and activist

Designing
public spaces

Creating a successful public space takes more than a love of Lego and SimCity!
There are many practical considerations, from design sense to drainage. A winning blueprint for a public space has many elements, most of which relate to the space's ability to attract people.

What makes a **great** public space?

Shared vision – Great public spaces aren't born from one person's imagination. Architects work in collaboration with urban planners, the people who manage a city's growth. Landscape architects design green spaces that complement the neighborhoods around them. If a space is to serve the public well, designers need to ask the government and the community what people need.

Beauty – People are more likely to spend time in a space that's pleasing to the eye. Not only should it look good from the inside, it must fit within its surroundings, too. A beautiful space that shows off the character of a city creates civic pride and draws tourists from around the world. But good looks aren't enough on their own. The space also needs to function well.

Sociability – Designers often refer to a space's sociability, or the way it brings people together. Just as a variety of crops makes for healthier soil, a well-designed space should attract a variety of people — of different ages, interests and backgrounds. If one group dominates, it will make others feel less welcome.

Comfort – No one sticks around for long when they're forced to stay on their feet or be exposed to the weather. A comfortable space makes people want to linger by providing places to sit and shelter from the sun, wind and rain. It must be clean and in good repair, with lots of trash cans and recycling bins to help people tidy up after themselves. And don't forget the restrooms!

Flexibility – Popular spaces are suitable for a range of activities. The same town square might host a farmer's market in the morning, be a popular lunch spot at midday, provide a place to do homework in the afternoon and host a concert in the evening.

Landmarks – When you imagine Paris, what do you picture? Probably the Eiffel Tower, the world's most visited landmark. On a grand scale, landmarks can help define a city. They create beautiful skylines and show off the talents of the world's greatest artists and architects. On a more practical level, they provide a place to get together. "Meet me at the park," you might say. "I'll be at the fountain."

Accessibility – A true public space should be accessible to everyone. That means wheelchair ramps and easy-to-navigate grounds that won't be difficult for people who are visually impaired or unsteady on their feet. The space must also be easy to get to from the surrounding areas, preferably by foot, bike or transit.

Safety – Great spaces attract lots of people, which goes a long way toward making them safe. Additionally, the space should be well lit with plenty of signage to help people get around with confidence.

Why do **public spaces** fail?

"It is difficult to design a space that will not attract people," the sociologist William H. Whyte wrote. "What is remarkable is how often this has been accomplished."

Let's start with four "ughs": ugly, uncomfortable, unwelcoming and unsafe. You know these places when you see them — they're usually empty. They look abandoned, possibly dangerous, on the brightest of days. Many seem more like drab passageways to the real public spaces beyond.

There are also plenty of spaces that look great at a glance, but the designers seem to have spent too much time on aesthetics, or appearances, and not enough thinking about how people will use them. "Don't walk on the grass," many of these spaces seem to say. "Keep your fingers off the monument."

Designers need to think about how a public space will feel and function when you're in it. For example, seating areas around the edge of a space tend to work only if there's an event happening in the middle. Otherwise, people can feel adrift. Unfortunately, seating and shelter are often eliminated to keep away undesirable people, such as the homeless. (If you don't provide a bench, no one can sleep on it, right?)

Some places are simply hard to find or access. They may have poorly marked entrances or be cut off from the flow of pedestrian traffic by busy roadways. What does it matter if a space is pretty if people don't know where it is? Or if they're reluctant to cross an intersection in order to get to it? That's why a simple set of steps on a busy street corner may be more crowded than the grandest of public space designs. In the end, what people value most is a place to sit, something to watch and a sense of belonging.

PEOPLE POWER

Strictly speaking, one of the most disputed public spaces in the United States isn't a public space at all. But the People's Park in Berkeley, California, is a prime example of the conflicts that can occur when a space isn't designed for a community.

In 1957, the University of California started buying 1.1 hectares (2.8 acres) of residential land for student housing, evicting homeowners in the process. By the time the sales were complete, the university had decided to use the land for parking and a playing field instead. In April 1969, frustrated students, merchants and residents decided to turn the badly maintained lot into a community park. Hundreds of people joined the effort. They planted trees, created gardens and installed playground equipment. Meanwhile, the university decided to proceed with its plans.

After a few tense weeks, Governor Ronald Reagan sent in the police, who installed a fence to keep people out of the park. A rally to protest the fence quickly turned violent. As the crowd doubled in size from 3000 to 6000 people, hundreds of police in full riot gear were brought in and the governor declared a state of emergency. Although freedom of assembly is denied during a state of emergency, a memorial service went ahead for a protestor who died of his injuries after clashing with police. The National Guard surrounded the crowd and dropped tear gas from a helicopter.

On May 30, 30 000 people — a third of the city — marched in protest. The occupation finally ended, but the park was an ongoing source of tension. Conflicts between the university, the locals and the police continued over the next three decades.

Today, the People's Park is still owned by the University of California, although it serves the community. The park includes gardens, a picnic area, a stage, a basketball court, a play area for children and seating. It has become a symbol of the turbulent social change of the 1960s, the value of urban parks, and the power of a public space to bring a community together.

Great **greens**

GUERRILLA GARDENING

Sean Canavan of London, England, is on the frontlines of a (ahem) growing movement known as guerrilla gardening. Often under cover of darkness, stealthy gardeners clean out unused or neglected plots of land and fill them with cheap but beautiful native plant species. Canavan, who has been blind for nearly a decade, surrounded the trees on his street with colorful flowers. Being able to work in the dark is one advantage to being blind, he has joked, although he no longer has to evade authorities. Canavan has been honored with an Exceptional People in Camden Award for his contribution to the community.

Great green spaces have all the elements of other successful public spaces — comfort, accessibility, beauty and function. Plants and trees provide shade on a hot day and homes for urban wildlife. Community gardens supply organic produce for local markets. They're a terrific place to learn about growing food, too!

Designing green spaces isn't always a walk in the park. Made of living materials, they require ongoing effort, and not all can be used year round. Lawns must be mowed, trees pruned, gardens planted and weeded. Playground equipment must meet exacting safety standards. And nature trails need regular grooming.

But the rewards of all that work go well beyond creating a place for people to throw a ball or make out on the grass. Green spaces also help clean the air by absorbing carbon dioxide, the pollutant most responsible for global warming. No wonder parks have been called "the lungs of the city" — they really are a breath of fresh air.

Al-Azhar Park may be one of the most breathtakingly beautiful parks on the planet, but for 500 years it was one impressive rubbish heap. It took 80 000 truckloads to clear out the debris and make way for the 30-hectare (74-acre) public space now located in the heart of historic Cairo, Egypt.

Before the park was built, the amount of green space per person was estimated to be the size of a footprint, one of the lowest such ratios in the world.

Today, the park includes an outsized playground built over the reservoirs that provide the city with fresh water.

And not only did the city gain a much-needed oasis, the excavation uncovered important artifacts, including the now restored 12th-century Ayyubid wall.

51

Living **history**

When you step onto a historic site, your imagination doesn't have to leap far to take you back in time. The sights, sounds, feel, even the smell of history surrounds you — it's in the floorboards of a Dawson City saloon or the dripping, cave-like tunnels of the Castillo de San Felipe de Barajas fortress in Cartagena des Indias, Colombia.

We often protect buildings because someone famous lived there or because the area was the background to significant historic events. But there is another, equally important reason to preserve historic spaces. Every era is defined by its architecture, including the present day, and we can learn a lot about our past by looking at the buildings around us.

Have you ever noticed those 1950s- and 1960s-era "Googie" buildings, such as Seattle's famous Space Needle? Over time, the "futuristic," space-age curves of Googie architecture have begun to look a little cartoonish — as if the designers lived up the street from the Incredibles. But these buildings represent a bold vision in an era when people were still captivated by the idea of space travel. In the same way, the car-inspired, art deco style of the Chrysler Building in New York City reflects America's love affair with the automobile in the 1920s.

Many great buildings have been lost over time — some knocked down, others destroyed by fire, war, natural disaster or neglect. And history has proven something again and again: you don't know what you have until it's gone.

THE NEW SEVEN WONDERS OF THE WORLD

So much of what we know about the ancient world is owed to the careful excavation and restoration of very old cities, monuments and religious sites. But ancient artifacts are as fragile as they are precious. Six of the original Seven Wonders of the World — the greatest human-made places of all time — have been destroyed by tragic disasters, such as earthquakes. Only the Great Pyramid of Giza survives.

In 2007, a private Swiss foundation sponsored an on-line contest to determine the New Seven Wonders of the World. More than 90 million people logged on to the Web site and voted for 21 short-listed places in an *American Idol*–style competition. An estimated 1.6 billion people tuned in for the televised results. The New Seven Wonders of the World are …

The ancient city of Machu Picchu, Peru

The ancient city of Petra, Jordan

The Colosseum, Rome, Italy

The Chichen Itza Pyramid, Yucatan Peninsula, Mexico

Christ the Redeemer statue, Rio de Janeiro, Brazil

The Taj Mahal, Agra, India

The Great Wall of China

Moving through spaces

A well-designed street and its sidewalks aren't just made for walking. They also host parades and road races. They're where we park our cars and bikes. Where we set out our recycling and junk for pick up, whether by the city or passersby. (In my neighborhood, placing something on the curb means "take it.") We decorate them with lights, planters and sidewalk chalk. We stop on them to chat with the people we bump into — friends, neighbors, people needing directions — often annoying other pedestrians trying to get by.

You've probably noticed that the older a neighborhood is, the narrower its streets are. That's because communities used to be designed around people, not cars. These old streets still work well as public spaces because they encourage human interaction. And the livelier the street, the more people are drawn to it.

Nowadays, North American cities are built for cars. Wide streets dominate and sidewalks aren't always built anymore. (Want to walk your dog after dark? By all means, take your life in your hands.) All this driving contributes to more car traffic pollution, a worldwide environmental crisis. Smog-related illnesses, such as asthma, are on the rise among youth, and dwindling resources have sent the cost of fuel skyrocketing. Yet, people refuse to get out of their cars.

What's the solution? Find other ways for people to get around — ways that are friendlier to people, cities and our lungs! One of the top reasons cited for not walking or cycling to work or school is safety. This problem could be addressed if cities included more bike lanes (especially in the downtown core), sidewalks in the suburbs

and pedestrian crossings on busy streets. Some people argue that these measures slow traffic to a crawl, but giving people alternatives to driving means fewer cars on the road. Besides, streets that are busy with pedestrian traffic are generally safer. When motorists are more mindful of the activity on the streets around them, it decreases the likelihood of accidents.

For those who need a lift, buses and subways have to run on time and follow enough routes to get people where they need to go quickly. Cash-strapped cities often claim that public transit is a chicken-and-egg situation: if you build it they will ride, but you need to ride so they can raise the money to build it. What if everyone committed to commuting on transit at least three times per week? Not only would that increase demand, it would give people a chance to see what works and doesn't work about the system, information you could share with your city councilor.

"Can you tell me how to get, how to get to...?"

In the late 19th and early 20th centuries, public life took up the entire street. Kids played right in the middle, while adults looked on. Want a more recent example? *Sesame Street!* When the program began in 1969, the set was designed to look like the perfect inner city street — with litter-free sidewalks, people on every stoop and rarely a car in sight.

Imagining the possibilities

These mean streets used to be designed around cars and other vehicles.

After some clever re-imagining that puts people first, both traffic and city life now go with the flow.

Wheels of change

One idea that has been gathering momentum is getting rid of cars altogether — at least in some places, some of the time. Car-free days give people in a designated area a break from vehicle traffic, a chance to cross a road without looking both ways. They free up the streets for markets and festivals and let people experience what a neighborhood would be like if cars were permanently restricted or banned.

Each September, more than 100 million people in fifteen hundred cities take part in International Car-Free Day, and many cities host car-free days throughout the year. Activists use car-free days to raise awareness of the environmental hazards of motor vehicle use and to promote alternative ways of getting around, such as cycling.

Europe has always been ahead of the curve when it comes to creating bicycle-friendly spaces. Since the first Bike Share program was launched in Amsterdam, the Netherlands, in the 1960s, similar programs have been launched all over the world. The concept is simple: a fleet of bikes is parked in racks around the city. Deposit a coin in the lock slot, remove the bike and cycle away. You'll get the coin back when you return the bike to another bike rack. Alternatively, you might pay a small fee or donate volunteer hours to the organizing body in exchange for keeping the same bike for a set period of time. Bike Share programs give people a fun and healthy way to explore a city without putting more cars on the road.

CRITICAL MASS

Started in San Francisco in 1992, thousands of cyclists take part in large monthly group rides through cities in dozens of countries. Naturally, getting swarmed by bicycles causes huge headaches for drivers, but the cyclists are unapologetic. The message? We don't block traffic, we *are* traffic. Critical Mass rides take place on the same day of each month, are open to people of all ages, and have no official organizers.

Every Sunday and during holidays, streets in downtown Bogotá, Colombia, are transformed into *ciclovías*, or "cycling streets." More than a million people cycle, walk and skate along routes where cars have been temporarily banned or restricted.

"Bikewatch" inspectors (think *Baywatch* lifeguards on wheels) ensure everyone stays safe.

At the sides of the road, fitness instructors lead aerobics and dance lessons from 20 temporary stages and food kiosks offer well-deserved refreshments.

Bogotá also has over 300 km (186 mi.) of *Ciclo-Rutas*, or bike lanes, one of the most extensive systems in the world.

59

HAIRCUTS BY CHILDREN

A scissor-wielding 8-year-old has just grabbed a handful of your hair. Nightmare or public performance art? The brainchild of the arts company Mammalian Diving Reflex, Haircuts by Children has been staged in Dublin, Sydney, Portland, New York, Vancouver and Toronto. By putting themselves, quite literally, into the hands of children (non-actors who have received some basic training by local hairstylists), participants and onlookers have a chance to think about how creative and competent kids can be, while allowing them to make mistakes (if you consider green hair or a wee bald spot to be a mistake).

Beautiful spaces

You don't need to be able to afford a Picasso to see amazing art. And you don't have to be Picasso to create and display art in a public space. "Public art" can refer to both art for the public and by the public, such as a theater performance in the park or a display of student paintings on a library wall.

Public art is free to all and, like public spaces themselves, showcases the richness and diversity of a culture. It is hard to measure its value in dollars and cents. How much would you pay for the pleasure of stepping off a subway car and being greeted by a bright mural or a busker playing your favorite tune?

Whether or not you can put a price tag on it, public art improves our quality of life in many ways. It provokes thought and discussion, and introduces people to artists' work. It highlights a country's or city's artistic traditions and may commemorate an important event or a person's life. It is nice to look at or listen to — except, of course, when it isn't. Controversy is often stirred when a city buys a work of abstract art that is not conventionally beautiful. The problem is, when it comes to art, one person's innovation can be another person's eyesore.

Soweto Mountain of Hope (SOMOHO)

The humble mountain on the edge of Soweto, South Africa, was once a crime-ridden dump ground.

Lead by environmentalist Mandla Mentoor, the surrounding communities have transformed a hillside into the Soweto Mountain of Hope, or SOMOHO — a clean, green haven filled with art, crafts and music.

The local water tower is now a community center for art workshops, dance and music lessons and stage productions.

Nothing goes to waste on SOMOHO. Local artists recycle materials into intricate baskets, bowls, beadwork, traditional masks and other creations. Old tires are used as flowerpots and rocks provide seating for group meetings and poetry readings.

The story of **graffiti**

People have been writing on walls for thousands of years, with examples dating back as far as Ancient Egypt, Rome and Pompeii. The word "graffiti" comes from the Greek word *graphein*, which means "to write." Modern graffiti artists call themselves graf-writers, though graffiti may include images.

Modern graffiti bloomed in New York City in the late 1960s. A messenger who went by the nickname Taki 183 (he lived on 183rd Street) "tagged" subway cars all over the city, inscribing his name with a marker. The idea spread rapidly after the *New York Times* profiled Taki, and young people began competitively tagging the city. Spray paint from aerosol cans made the job easier and highly stylized lettering became the mainstay of the art form.

These days, graffiti can be colorful and elaborate, but cities are still blanketed by simple tags. The graf-writers' tag was, and still is, the story on the wall. It says: "I was here."

"OH NO! MY PROPERTY VALUE JUST WENT DOWN!"

– from a mural in downtown Toronto created by the city's Graffiti Transformation Program

Street **art** or street **crime**?

Graffiti has provided inspiration for many other art forms, from fashion to comic books, and is an important part of hip-hop culture. But for many people graffiti is vandalism, plain and simple. It suffers from its association with gangs, for whom space is everything: graffiti is how they mark their territory.

Not surprisingly, many business owners loathe graffiti. It hurts property values and is a royal pain to remove. And let's face it, not all graf-writers are equally good at their trade. Many say they won't write on private property or important public spaces, such as museum walls or monuments, but clearly there are people who do.

For years, lawmakers have tried to deter graf-writers with the threat of hefty fines and even jail time. Some cities are becoming more proactive, creating programs that put them to work for the public good. Toronto has initiated a Graffiti Transformation Program, which hires young artists to remove graffiti and resurface walls with murals. More than 400 murals now cover the city throughout the downtown core.

Ironically, if graf-writers didn't break the law, we might not know just how many people, and youth in particular, need an outlet for their artistic expression — or what a terrible waste of space a blank wall can be.

Art vs. ads

POLLUTION SOLUTION

In 2007, the mayor of São Paulo, Brazil, decided enough was enough. Mayor Gilberto Kassab introduced the Clean City Law, which banned all outdoor advertising, in any form, in this city of 11 million people, calling it "visual pollution." The law brought down more than 8000 billboards, as well as transit ads and posters. Privately owned spaces, such as storefronts, were limited to signs no bigger than 1.5 m (5 ft.) for every 10 m (33 ft.) of frontage. Some people opposed the ban, complaining of the high cost of removing ads. They also pointed out the loss of millions of dollars in ad revenue and potentially thousands of jobs. Nevertheless, 70% of the city's inhabitants approved of the ban, and some former ad spaces are now used for community information bulletins.

If graffiti is an eyesore, what do you call a vodka ad?

We're so used to seeing advertising and logos everywhere that you might not notice just how much public space is for sale. The sun sets behind enormous billboards, while billboard trucks drive their messages down the streets. Transit vehicles are covered with ads; subway stations flash commercials on monitors and even their floors may be slicked with marketing messages.

Like renting out a public space for a film shoot, cities sell ad space to the private sector in order to raise money — often for much-needed public programs. But while the public might be consulted before the city invests in public art, it has little or no say over the content of advertising.

At the same time, some cities are cracking down on those who help themselves to free advertising. Taping or gluing posters to telephone poles is one of the cheapest and most effective ways to get the word out about things like community meetings and music performances. Some people see postering as a form of self-expression, a way of communicating with others and creating art for public display. Others, like Toronto city councilor Denzil Minnan-Wong, call it "pollution and litter."

Minnan-Wong found himself at odds with the local music scene when Toronto introduced a new anti-postering bylaw. Many musicians, including Jason Collett, a member of the collective Broken Social Scene, protested the bylaw. "[Postering] is a simple way of connecting to your neighborhood," he explains, "whether it's a yard sale, lost cat or some young band's upcoming show." Collett says he has put up posters himself and found them to be effective.

The city tried to broker a compromise by decreeing that posters may go up but may not overlap and must come down within five days. Activists continue to protest the bylaw, arguing that it is too hard to enforce.

Delettering the public space

In 2005, Austrian artists Christoph Steinbrener and Rainer Dempf drew attention to the ads covering every inch of available space in Vienna — by erasing them. In an enormous art installation called *Delete!: Delettering Public Space*, all of the advertising and logos on a busy shopping street were replaced with bright yellow plastic and foil for two weeks. What might your city look like with no advertising or logos in its public spaces?

How would **you** build it?

You've been hired to design a new town square, and community groups have given you a wish list of features they'd like the space to include. How many of the requests can you accommodate? Photocopy this basic town square, then cut out and arrange the icons provided (and design your own) to meet the community's needs. You could even build a 3-D model. Just keep in mind all the elements shared by great pubic spaces.

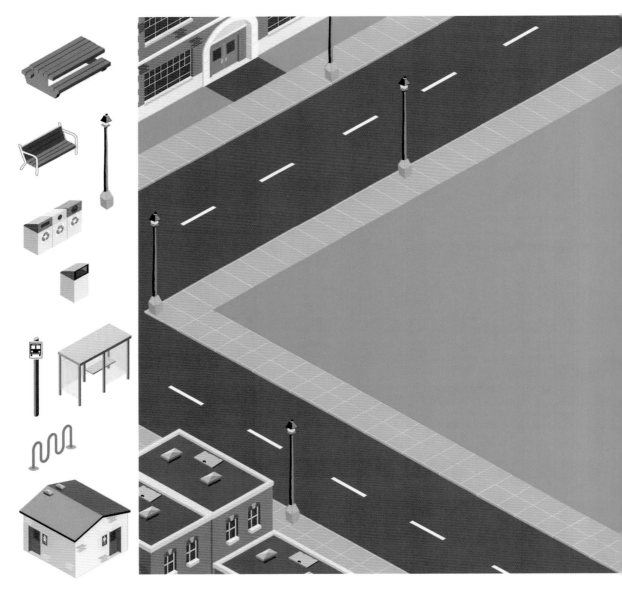

Community Wish List

- Places to sit
- Shade
- Places to walk
- Good lighting

- Easy access from the street
- Green areas (e.g., flowerbeds)
- Public art (e.g., sculptures)
- Skating rink or skateboarding area

- A wall for graffiti, a mural or a community message board
- Open space for a farmers' market, concerts and festivals
- Washrooms

"The world belongs to the energetic."
— Ralph Waldo Emerson, philosopher and poet

Fighting for public space

Remember, public space is yours. You have every right to get pissed off about sold space, ugly space, unused space and wasted space. But ownership comes with responsibility, and that means doing something when you see a problem.

Steal this **idea**

Whether it's writing a letter to your local paper or inviting a speaker to talk to your school or community group, small actions can lead the way to big changes. We asked public space advocates for positive ways you can raise awareness about the issues that are important to you and begin changing your community for the better.

Matthew Johnson, Media Awareness Network

Putting the Public Back in Public School

Schools are supposed to be public spaces, but more and more advertisers are using them to target youth. Corporations know just how much time kids spend at school, whether in class, in after-school activities or just hanging out with their friends, and they don't want to pass up a chance to reach them there. Here are some things you can do to keep commercials and other advertising materials out of your school:

Develop an ad-free policy

Your student council and parent council can work together to create new or improved policies about advertising in your school. If your school already has a corporate partnership, encourage your student and parent councils to look at ways of minimizing the ad presence in school.

Start a no logo day at school

Challenge students to come to school without any logos on their clothing, bags, etc. They'll be surprised at how hard it is just to get dressed!

Hold an advertising treasure hunt

Get students to make a list of all the logos and other advertising materials in the school (soft drink machines, sponsored educational materials, etc.).

Organize an advertising diary project

Have people record every ad and commercial message they see or hear, from the moment they wake up until they go to bed. Don't forget to include on-line ads!

Write a letter

Your local newspaper is a great place to get the word out about the commercialization of schools. Invite a reporter to your No Logo Day or Advertising Treasure Hunt.

Finally, encourage media education at your school. The best antidote to advertising and commercialization is to learn to recognize messages and to think critically about them.

Andrew Pask, Vancouver Public Space Network

Join the Fight for Public Space

Does your city or town have a public space group? Why not ring 'em up or send an e-mail to find out how to join? Believe me, they're always looking for extra help. If there isn't already a group, consider starting one. Put the word out and call a meeting — you can even go solo. It doesn't matter if your "crew" is one person or a hundred, there's much you can do.

Start by naming all of the public space issues that you're concerned about. They might include a messy beach, junk food vending machines in your school or advertising on buses. Then, name all the public spaces that are important to you, such as the cool ravine near your home, your favorite skateboard park or a great graffiti wall. Congratulations, you've just created a list of places where you can get your hands dirty!

Next up, plan your approach. In very broad terms, you may want to have a "fun" approach and a "serious" approach. That way, you'll get a reputation for being a light-hearted group that other youth will want to join — and at the same time, get things done.

The fun stuff is about celebrating public spaces, encouraging people to use them and creating a sense of community. You could stage an event, such as holding a community picnic, or cover a space with chalk drawings or paintings. (Use washable paint so your good intentions don't backfire.)

On the serious side, set goals and break down the steps toward taking action to promote or protect your favorite public spaces. Be sure to do some research before you act. Find out more about the issue, its history and who it affects. Once you're informed, speak up! Make a brochure, put up posters or write a letter to the local newspaper. Circulate a petition, call a community meeting or create a Web site.

Most importantly, never assume that people actually know about your concerns or that somebody else is doing something. With any issue, it always takes at least one person to flag it in the first place. Maybe that person will be you!

ANDREW'S TIP: WHEN CONTACTING A LOCAL GOVERNMENT REPRESENTATIVE, DON'T BE SHY ABOUT ASKING QUESTIONS: PUBLIC OFFICIALS ARE THERE TO SERVE THE PUBLIC, AND THAT MEANS KIDS, TOO. IF SOMETHING ABOUT THE SITUATION DOESN'T MAKE SENSE, THEN SAY AS MUCH! OFTENTIMES, IT DOESN'T MAKE SENSE TO THOSE IN CHARGE, EITHER. IF YOU PRESS A LITTLE, YOU MAY PROVOKE A THOUGHTFUL DISCUSSION THAT LEADS TO AGREEMENT.

56 Things you can do in a public park: Walk **Jog** Run **Wheel** Rollerblade **Bicycle** Wade in a pool **Splash in a** ➔

LISA'S TIP:
HOW ABOUT ENCOURAGING YOUR LIBRARY TO PURCHASE THE MUSIC OF LOCAL ARTISTS? YOU COULD THEN OFFER A FREE CONCERT TO PROMOTE THE COLLECTION.

Lisa Heggum, Youth Collections Librarian, Toronto Public Library

The Public Library: Making It Yours

The public library is your space to help shape. You can create areas (physical and virtual) that are welcoming, safe and respectful to youth; fill them with interesting and relevant collections (books, music, movies and games); and plan all kinds of related programs. How? Many libraries have youth advisory groups you can join. If your local library doesn't have one, why not get one started? Here are some pointers for running a successful group:

• get a librarian on board who's a strong youth advocate
• recruit members who reflect the diversity of your community
• keep the group a manageable size
• schedule regular meetings
• create meeting agendas and record your thoughts and recommendations
• start with a manageable project and build momentum
• promote the things you plan
• work with community agencies who share similar goals
• thank and recognize members for their contributions
• serve snacks!

You'll be amazed by the energy of your group and the things you can accomplish together. For example, you might run a fine-forgiveness program for youth to encourage them to return to the library or create a great new Web site or blog that your friends actually visit and contribute to. You could start a manga or anime club or hold fundraisers to buy equipment to run a gaming tournament.

The possibilities are endless. From book clubs to open mics, craft circles to sleepovers (yes, sleepovers at the library!), there are all sorts of possibilities and you can help make them happen.

puddle Birdwatch **Feed the wildlife** Get chased by a swan **Have a picnic** Have a barbeque **Play fetch with a dog** Watch the dogs play **Watch a toddler**

Cindy Carlson,
Hampton Youth Commission

Get a Voice at City Hall

In Hampton, Virginia, twenty-five teens serve as the voice for youth in municipal government. Working with the city council, the Hampton Youth Commission (HYC) has launched two main projects around public space: the Hampton Teen Center, a state-of-the-art teen facility ten years in the making; and the Youth-Friendly Guidebook, which lists youth-friendly stores, businesses and community centers compiled by "secret shoppers" who visited and evaluated them. These are just two examples of ways that teens can benefit a community when given a chance to be part of the solution.

Starting a youth commission is a big job: it requires planning, time and money. You might want to start by proposing a pilot project to your city or town council. If it is successful, you could then talk about establishing a permanent role for teens at city hall.

For instance, suppose your hometown is facing a challenge with bicycle-related injuries. A youth group working with the city could

• spend a Saturday morning teaching bicycle safety to children at a bike rodeo.

• advise city planners on dangerous intersections or new bike route designs (if your city already has a citizens' advisory committee for bike issues, ask about adding a voice for youth to the group).

• help research, write and propose a new bicycle ordinance (a regulation or law) for the city.

CINDY'S TIP: DOES YOUR LIBRARY OR COMMUNITY CENTER HAVE A YOUTH ADVISORY GROUP? THEY MAY BE ABLE TO SHARE PRACTICAL ADVICE, FROM SETTING GOALS TO DEALING WITH PEOPLE IN AUTHORITY.

learn to walk Watch old people watching young people **Read a book** Listen to your iPod **Listen to an outdoor concert** Watch the sun set **Watch the**

73

Kevin Bracken and Lori Kufner, Newmindspace

Celebrating Public Spaces

How do we fight for public space? Gigantic pillow fights, water balloon wars and cardboard tube battles!

Turning your community into a massive playground is an easy and fun way to celebrate public spaces. We call it "metromorphosis," or "the art of city transformation." We've partied on subway cars with portable speakers, organized huge bubble-blowing parties and massive games of capture the flag, and coordinated spontaneous parades with marching bands and costumes. In most cases, you shouldn't have to get a permit or formal permission —

public assembling is a human right. All you need are some friends, an Internet connection and an idea for an event.

Where? Any public space will do, but don't use parks, please. Not only will you protect them from litter, but you'll also protect your event from banality. Most events like this in parks are boring, probably because you can't count on having a lot of people there. Often it's better to go where people are — then you can invite them to join in!

When? We've always preferred Saturday afternoons because they ensure a greater diversity of ages (parents and children tend to skip nighttime events) and that gives the

event a warmer feeling. Also, sunlight makes it easier to photograph all those memorable moments.

How? Web-based groups, such as Yahoo and Google, or a mailing program, such as Dada Mail (software) or YMLP (service), get the word out fast. You can post a sign-up link on your Web site, social networking sites and/or blog, and your e-mail list will grow organically from there. Of course, Facebook is another super-quick way to reach all your friends.

Now you are armed with the tools you need to turn public spaces into places you want to party! What are you waiting for? Go out and play!

sun rise Take photographs **Paint a picture** Write a poem **Work on your laptop** Read a book **Fall asleep on the grass** Meet someone new **Smooch**

Matthew Blackett, Spacing Magazine

How to Host a Successful Fundraiser

You've joined a group, chosen your cause and are ready to fight for public space. But first you need money to pay for things like gardening or poster-making supplies. You may be able to apply for grants from a nonprofit foundation or the government, but the quickest way to raise cash is a fundraising event.

There are three skills you need to host a successful fundraiser: organization, organization and organization. If you're going to ask people to support your cause, do it right by planning well in advance and leaving no detail overlooked. They're also going to expect something for their money. Games and quizzes encourage people to interact with one another. Speeches will let everyone know how you plan to use the funds you raise. Ask local businesses to donate products that can be raffled off during the event. Live entertainment, such as bands or DJs, may attract people who are fans of the act and not (yet) aware of you. We like to call this cross-pollination.

The next step is to find a venue. There are several things to consider, including how suitable it is for your event. Is there a stage? Are there tables and chairs? Can you set up an LCD projector or speakers? It also needs to be easy to get to. Is it near public transit? Are there parking spaces nearby? How many people do you expect to attend? We prefer a smaller venue over a cavernous place that'll look empty even if everyone shows up.

Once the details are set, promote your event like crazy! You might hook up with another group that shares your goals and can advertise the event through their newsletter or Web site. They may also be able to lend some volunteers — people to sell tickets in advance and at the door, hand out information materials, help clean up, etc. And if you have merchandise like T-shirts or buttons, make sure to have lots to sell!

If you make the effort, a fundraiser is not only a great way to raise money but to spread the word about public space, get people to join your cause and have fun!

MATHEW'S TIP: BEFORE YOU BOOK A VENUE, GET THE COST IN WRITING AND ADD IT TO YOUR OTHER EXPENSES. THIS WILL HELP YOU FIGURE OUT HOW MANY TICKETS YOU NEED TO SELL BEFORE YOU START MAKING A PROFIT.

Fall in love **Get married** Break up **Talk to your friends** Play chess or checkers **Play croquet, catch, soccer or football** Do tai chi **Or watch** ➡

75

Dan Burden, Walkable Communities

Lead the Way

Young people often have the best insights into what has gone or is going wrong with public spaces, but they are rarely asked. Here are just a few examples of ways youth can show community leaders how to make public spaces better for walking, biking and playing:

In Glace Bay, Nova Scotia, youth played an important role in improving their town's walking and biking routes. Members of a youth action committee took a group of transportation consultants on a walkabout of their town. Each member led the group on a segment of the walk, then asked the consultants to rate each area on a scale of one to ten and explain their ratings. They also offered their own recommendations for change.

In Delft, the Netherlands, young people learned the practice of "rubber band planning" to discover the best ways to walk or bike to important places. Rubber band planning uses an aerial map, pins and stretchable string to track the best travel routes according to local people. The planning reveals where public works projects are needed, such as adding or improving walkways, trails and pedestrian crossings.

In Melbourne, Australia, students helped kick off a national conference called "Let Kids Live" by inviting hundreds of elected leaders, planners, architects, police and others to hear messages developed and delivered by the youth of the city on what was missing from their lives. Their eloquent, from-the-heart suggestions had a huge impact, reminding the people in charge of budgets and planning just how important public spaces are to youth.

You, too, can help turn a town around. Take a cue from these kids, who visualized better futures then took the initiative to start re-making their public spaces.

DAN'S TIP: WANT TO DRAW ATTENTION TO A PROBLEM IN YOUR TOWN? ORGANIZE A WALKING OR BIKING TOUR WITH COMMUNITY MEMBERS, MEDIA AND ELECTED LEADERS.

those amazingly fit seniors do it Snowshoe **Ski** Build a snowman **Have a snowball fight** Put on an outdoor play **Watch an outdoor play**

76

Acknowledgments

The research for this vast topic involved far too much reading (and loitering in lovely spaces) to provide a complete list of sources here, but I would like to offer my sincere thanks to those who made special contributions to this book.

Thank you to our Chapter Four contributors — Matthew Blackett, Kevin Bracken, Dan Burden, Cindy Carlson, Lisa Heggum, Matthew Johnson, Lori Kufner and Andrew Pask — who not only provided wonderful advice for our readers, but also informed my research and writing through interviews and the example of their good own works.

For supplying expert opinions, facts and support, I am much obliged to Rick Book, Lena Coakley, Jason Collett, Heather Johnson, the International Council of Shopping Centers, Isabelle Lecroart, Dylan Reid, Kathy Stinson, Darren Wershler and Paula Wing.

Thank you to the young readers who offered their thoughts and feedback, especially Nancy Bowe's grade nine students at Bicentennial School in Dartmouth, Nova Scotia, whose writings about public space told me we were on the right track.

Special thanks to the Jane Jacobs Estate, Bob Dylan, George Radwanski and Ray Oldenburg for permission to reprint quotations and for the respective bodies of work that so influenced this book.

I am very grateful to Karen Li for suggesting this project and applying her awesomeness to it, and to Marc Ngui and Karen Powers for making it beautiful.

Finally, thank you to my family and friends. I'm going to single out Rachael, Heather and Christine — because you remember the sandpit and the parking lot and because we are still very good at doing nothing together.

Hold a day camp **Join the Friends of the Park organization** Create a Friends of the Park organization **Suggest establishing a community** ➜

Glossary

Note: Some words defined within the book do not appear in the glossary.

accessibility – the degree to which a space can be entered by all people, including those with wheelchairs, walkers and strollers

activists / activism – the practice of taking action to create political or social change

agora – a public area where people gathered in ancient Greece

architect / architecture – the profession of designing buildings and other structures

avatar – in an on-line or video game: a character or symbol that represents a participant

bylaws – a local law set by a municipal government, such as a city council

civic pride – pride in one's city or town

civil disobedience – deliberately breaking the law to protest a law that is considered unjust or to bring attention to an issue

Closed Circuit Television (CCTV) – video cameras that record and transmit images to a control room in order to monitor public activity

Commercial (vs. nonprofit) – relating to commerce or business

density (of a space) – the number of people who live within a specific geographical area

freedom of assembly / association – the right of individuals to come together as a group and express, promote or defend their common interests

green spaces – public spaces featuring land covered with plants, such as grass or trees

loitering – to be idle or spend time in a space with no specific purpose; hanging out

media education – knowledge and understanding of types of communications that reach large numbers of people, including television, radio, newspapers, advertising and the internet

nonprofit / not-for-profit – an organization whose activities are not aimed at earning a profit and often serve the public good

personal space – the space between an individual and other people

petition – a request for change or action, usually containing the signatures of people who support the request

postering – putting posters on telephone poles, walls, garbage cans and other items

proxemics – the study of spaces between people as they interact with one another

private space – spaces that are owned by individuals or companies, not the public

public property – land or buildings owned by the public, usually in a government's name

public space – a space that is owned by the public

public transit – transportation for moving the public, such as buses and subways, funded by government

social spaces – public or private spaces where people come together

suburbs / suburban – residential areas (places where people live) on the outskirts of the city

tag – a graf-writer's signature

urban – relating to a city

urban planning – the designing of cities or towns

youth commission / youth advisory group – a group of children or teenagers who advise on matters relating to youth concerns, ideas and programs

garden Or a farmers' market **Or a greenhouse** Or a playground **Or improve the existing garden, market, greenhouse or playground** Create

Index

an off-leash area for dogs **Or put a fence around the existing off-leash area** Help weed the park **And plant new things for next year**